Fashion changes, but style endures.
—COCO CHANEL

IN A TIME WHEN
CHILDREN WERE SEEN AND NOT HEARD,
ALONG CAME COCO—A LITTLE FRENCH GIRL
WITH AN EYE FOR STYLE, A TALENT FOR SEWING,
AND A VERY, VERY BIG IMAGINATION.

For my dear parents, Evelyn and Larry.
And for Ronnie, with love and
thanks, and our children: Ben, Sophie,
Jasmine, and Dylan,

—E.B.

The art for this book was created with watercolor, brush, and ink.

Cataloging-in-Publication Data has been applied for and
may be obtained from the Library of Congress.

ISBN 978-1-4197-3425-0

Text and illustration copyright © 2019 Eva Byrne
Book design by Pamela Notarantonio

Printed and bound in China
10 9 8 7 6 5 4 3 2 1

Abrams Books for Young Readers are available at special discounts when
purchased in quantity for premiums and promotions as well as fundraising
or educational use. Special editions can also be created to specification.
For details, contact specialsales@abramsbooks.com or the address below.

Abrams® is a registered trademark of Harry N. Abrams, Inc.

ABRAMS The Art of Books
195 Broadway, New York, NY 10007
abramsbooks.com

EVA BYRNE

Along Came COCO

A Story About COCO CHANEL

ABRAMS BOOKS FOR YOUNG READERS · *New York*

Coco Chanel was born in France in 1883. Coco's early days were spent not in the chic city of Paris, but in a strict convent tucked away in the French countryside. Life in a French orphanage was never going to be a fashionable affair.

But Coco always tried her best to be a little different. In her dreams, she imagined a new way of doing things.

Coco loved to watch the nuns as they seemed to glide about the convent in their black-and-white habits, looking so dramatic and mysterious.

She wanted to be dramatic and mysterious, too.

It was in the convent where Coco learned the sewing skills that would later make her famous. But in the meantime, she created charming little dolls for her friends out of scraps of leftover material. She entertained herself with extravagant stories and fabulous dreams for her future.

Coco was not so fabulous at following the rules . . . which was a pity, because nuns love rules.

One of the rules of the time was that hair must be brushed with one hundred strokes per day. All the curlyheads, the straight-as-a-pin heads, and the wavy and frizzy heads brushed until their arms were sore.

What a waste of a girl's time, thought Coco.
She imagined, *One day, I will cut my hair so short,*
I will barely need to brush it at all!

"No more daydreaming, young
mademoiselle. Rules are rules.
Keep brushing!"

As a treat, Coco was allowed to visit her grandparents in Moulins.

Together with her best friend, Aunt Adrienne, she watched the elegant women stroll by without a care in the world. She wanted to be just like them. She imagined a life far away from the discipline of the convent.

While visiting in Varennes, Coco watched as her Aunt Louise transformed storebought hats into eye-catching creations using ribbons, feathers, and flowers.

Coco had just caught a glimpse into her future.
She knew she could make hats, too.

So as soon as she was old enough, Coco packed
her sewing kit and waved goodbye to the convent.

Au revoir, darlings!

With the help of a dear friend, Coco opened a millinery shop in Paris. Coco's hats were different from the large, floppy hats decorated with birds' nests and butterflies that women were used to. Coco's hats were practical and easy to wear.

Finally, Coco was free to be herself. She took inspiration from all she saw around her. Inspired by the stripy tops of the local fishermen, she sewed her own version.

Coco opened another shop in the resort town of Deauville. The summer of 1914 was a hot one, so when Coco noticed the light, loose trousers worn by the messenger boys, she had an idea. She imagined that girls should be comfortable in the heat, too. And *voilà*!

A very stylish and modest swimsuit appeared on the beach.

Not everyone was impressed. But Coco didn't mind. She created clothes as she needed them. She was one of the first designers who knew exactly what women wanted.

Soon Aunt Adrienne and her friends were lining up to wear Coco's latest creations.

Coco's style was so fresh and exciting. In Coco's hands, a man's sporty sweater became a chic lady's cardigan. Coco even added pockets, freeing women's hands—a first for women's clothing. *Ooh-la-la!*

Coco's shop in Paris was a success. It was so successful that she bought the whole building at 31 rue Cambon and turned it into one of the most fashionable addresses in Paris. She sold dresses and jewelry, as well as her hats. Life had certainly changed since the convent!

When Coco wasn't working, she went to the ballet and the theater with friends. One afternoon, she was getting ready for the opera, when . . .

. . . disaster struck!

A gas lamp exploded in her
dressing room, destroying
her pink dress and burning
her hair. She was covered
in soot, and the smell of
burned hair was awful.

But there was no way Coco
was going to miss the opera!

Grabbing scissors, Coco
cut her hair and asked her
maid to finish the job.

Her new, short hair sprang out all at once
from around her face, different and delightful!

Now that Coco had fixed her hair, she needed to get dressed! But another rule of the time was that women should wear corsets. *C'est terrible!*

Imagine a very wide belt tied around your waist and laced tightly at the back. Now add some whalebones at the front and sides just to make sure it's as stiff as it can possibly get. Don't let the silk-covered buttons and lace ribbons fool you. There was nothing pretty about wearing a corset.

And don't worry about breathing.
That's what smelling salts are for.

As for fainting, well, there are fainting couches for that!

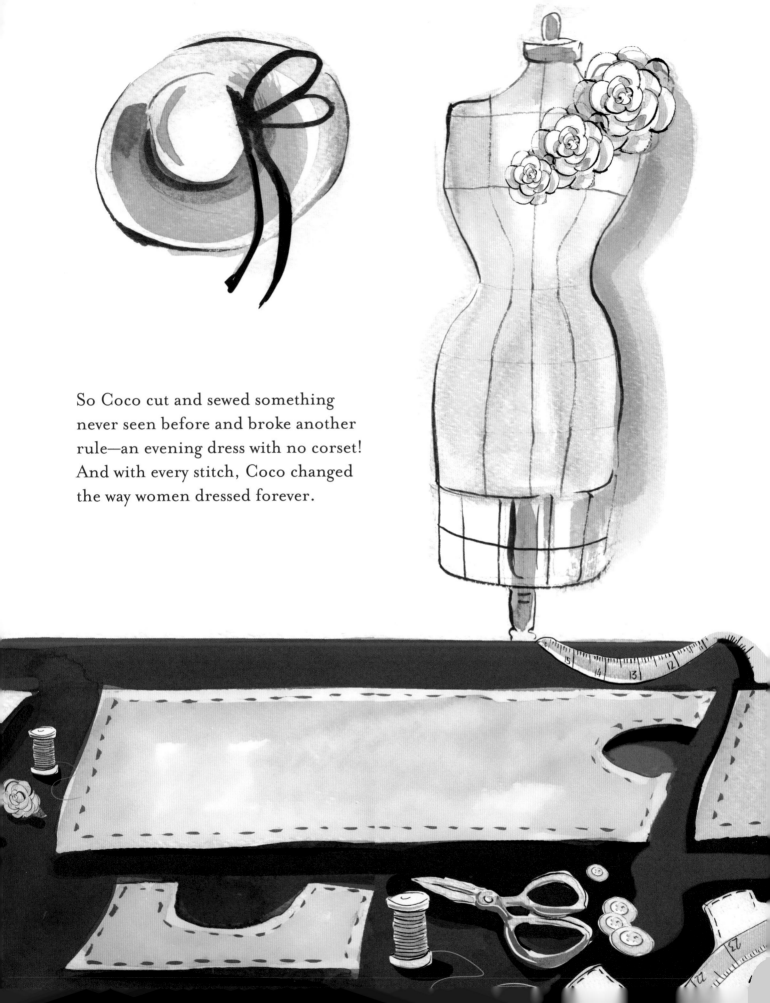

So Coco cut and sewed something
never seen before and broke another
rule—an evening dress with no corset!
And with every stitch, Coco changed
the way women dressed forever.

Breathtaking in its simplicity,
dramatic in its effect, a little
black dress was born. Coco
dreamed that all women
should have a black dress.
That evening at the opera,
Coco was the belle of the ball.

C'est chic!
C'est magnifique!
C'est fantastique!

As for corsets, smelling salts,
and fainting couches . . .
well, they became so last
season, darling!

*C'est
Coco!*

HAS THERE EVER BEEN
A LITTLE FRENCH GIRL
WITH SUCH A BIG IMAGINATION
WHO HAS MADE BREAKING THE RULES
LOOK SO GOOD?

About Coco Chanel

Gabrielle "Coco" Chanel was born on August 19, 1883, in France. At age twelve she was sent to a convent that ran an orphanage for girls, and it was there that she learned to sew. After finishing school, she became a seamstress, a hatmaker, and later, one of the most famous fashion designers the world has ever seen. Some of her innovations include dresses without corsets, the jersey dress, the nautical-inspired striped shirt, women's loose trousers, handbags with straps, cardigan sweaters with pockets, and the perfume Chanel No. 5. Chanel's designs were simple and chic and allowed women a newfound comfort and liberation—they could accomplish their daily tasks without their clothes getting in the way *and* without sacrificing style. Chanel died on January 10, 1971, in Paris.

Author's Note

From Coco Chanel to the person who works at my local bakery, people's stories have always fascinated me. How do people come to be who they are? How did a little French girl—born into poverty during a time when women were denied the right to vote or the right to own property—rise to become a cultural and fashion icon whose name is synonymous with style and luxury? For Coco, it was due to her imagination and sheer determination. As she once said, "I decided who I wanted to be, and that is who I am."

Coco's wild imagination is also what made telling her story so difficult. She was known for contradicting details about her humble origins and embellishing stories throughout her life, so it was challenging to distinguish her facts from her fiction. Some of the details I encountered about her life were not inspiring but instead truly despairing.

I've stared at the few photographs of Coco Chanel as a young woman trying to understand her, looking for clues in her frank gaze or in her sometimes mischievous expression. But the mystery remains. What I do know is that she was not afraid to do things differently. And so, I've tried to tell the story of Coco the innovator in a way I think she would have enjoyed—with the embellishments she might have dreamed up and a little extra *ooh-la-la* . . .

Selected Bibliography

Chaney, Lisa. *Chanel: An Intimate Life.* New York: Penguin Books, 2011.

Charles-Roux, Edmonde. *The World of Coco Chanel: Friends, Fashion, Fame.* London: Thames & Hudson, 2005.

Madsen, Axel. *Chanel: A Woman of Her Own.* New York: Henry Holt and Company, 1990.

Matthews, Elizabeth. *Different Like Coco.* Cambridge, MA: Candlewick Press, 2007.

Morand, Paul. *The Allure of Chanel.* London: Pushkin Press, 2008.

Mulvey, Kate, and Melisssa Richards. *Decades of Beauty: The Changing Image of Women 1890s–1990s.* New York: Checkmark Books, 1998.

Picardie, Justine. *Coco Chanel: The Legend and the Life.* New York: HarperCollins Publishers, 2010.

Pocket Coco Chanel Wisdom: Witty Quotes and Wise Words from a Fashion Icon. London: Hardie Grant Books, 2017.

Rubin, Susan Goldman. *Coco Chanel: Pearls, Perfume, and the Little Black Dress.* New York: Abrams Books for Young Readers, 2018.